COUNTRIES OF THE WORLD

Peru

by Monika Davies

BLASTOFF! READERS

BELLWETHER MEDIA • MINNEAPOLIS, MN

Blastoff! Readers are carefully developed by literacy experts to build reading stamina and move students toward fluency by combining standards-based content with developmentally appropriate text.

 **Level 1** provides the most support through repetition of high-frequency words, light text, predictable sentence patterns, and strong visual support.

 **Level 2** offers early readers a bit more challenge through varied sentences, increased text load, and text-supportive special features.

 **Level 3** advances early-fluent readers toward fluency through increased text load, less reliance on photos, advancing concepts, longer sentences, and more complex special features.

★ Blastoff! Universe

Reading Level

This edition first published in 2024 by Bellwether Media, Inc.

No part of this publication may be reproduced in whole or in part without written permission of the publisher. For information regarding permission, write to Bellwether Media, Inc., Attention: Permissions Department, 6012 Blue Circle Drive, Minnetonka, MN 55343.

Library of Congress Cataloging-in-Publication Data

Names: Davies, Monika, author.
Title: Peru / by Monika Davies.
Description: Minneapolis, MN : Bellwether Media, Inc., 2024. | Series: Blastoff! Readers : countries of the world | Includes bibliographical references and index. | Audience: Ages 5-8 | Audience: Grades 2-3 | Summary: "Relevant images match informative text in this introduction to Peru. Intended for students in kindergarten through third grade"– Provided by publisher.
Identifiers: LCCN 2023003650 (print) | LCCN 2023003651 (ebook) | ISBN 9798886874303 (library binding) | ISBN 9798886876185 (ebook)
Subjects: LCSH: Peru–Juvenile literature.
Classification: LCC F3408.5 .D38 2024 (print) | LCC F3408.5 (ebook) | DDC 985–dc23/eng/20230201
LC record available at https://lccn.loc.gov/2023003650
LC ebook record available at https://lccn.loc.gov/2023003651

Text copyright © 2024 by Bellwether Media, Inc. BLASTOFF! READERS and associated logos are trademarks and/or registered trademarks of Bellwether Media, Inc.

Editor: Rebecca Sabelko   Designer: Gabriel Hilger

Printed in the United States of America, North Mankato, MN.

Table of Contents

All About Peru	4
Land and Animals	6
Life in Peru	12
Peru Facts	20
Glossary	22
To Learn More	23
Index	24

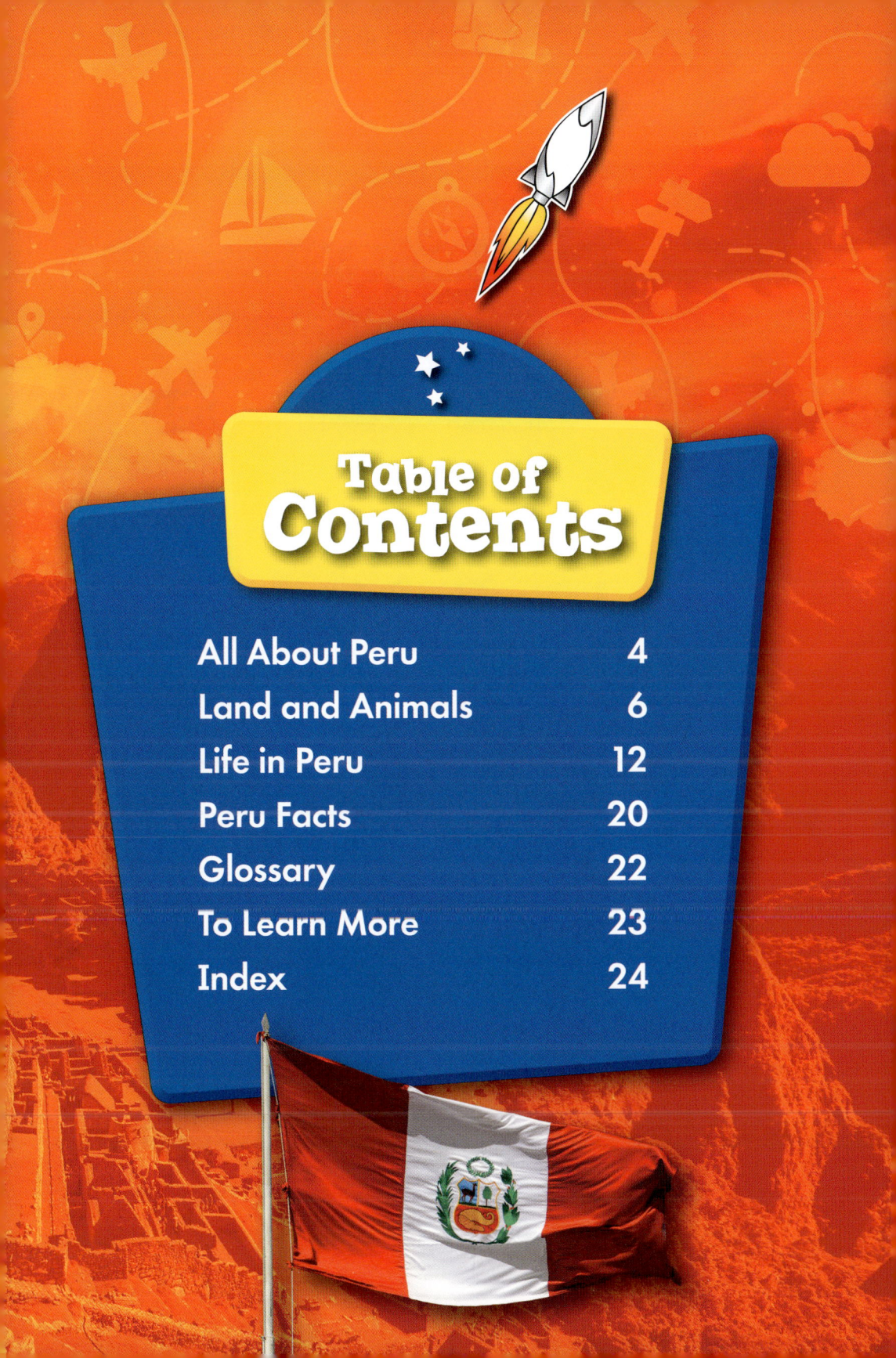

All About Peru

Lima

Peru is in South America. It lies next to the Pacific Ocean. The country's capital is Lima.

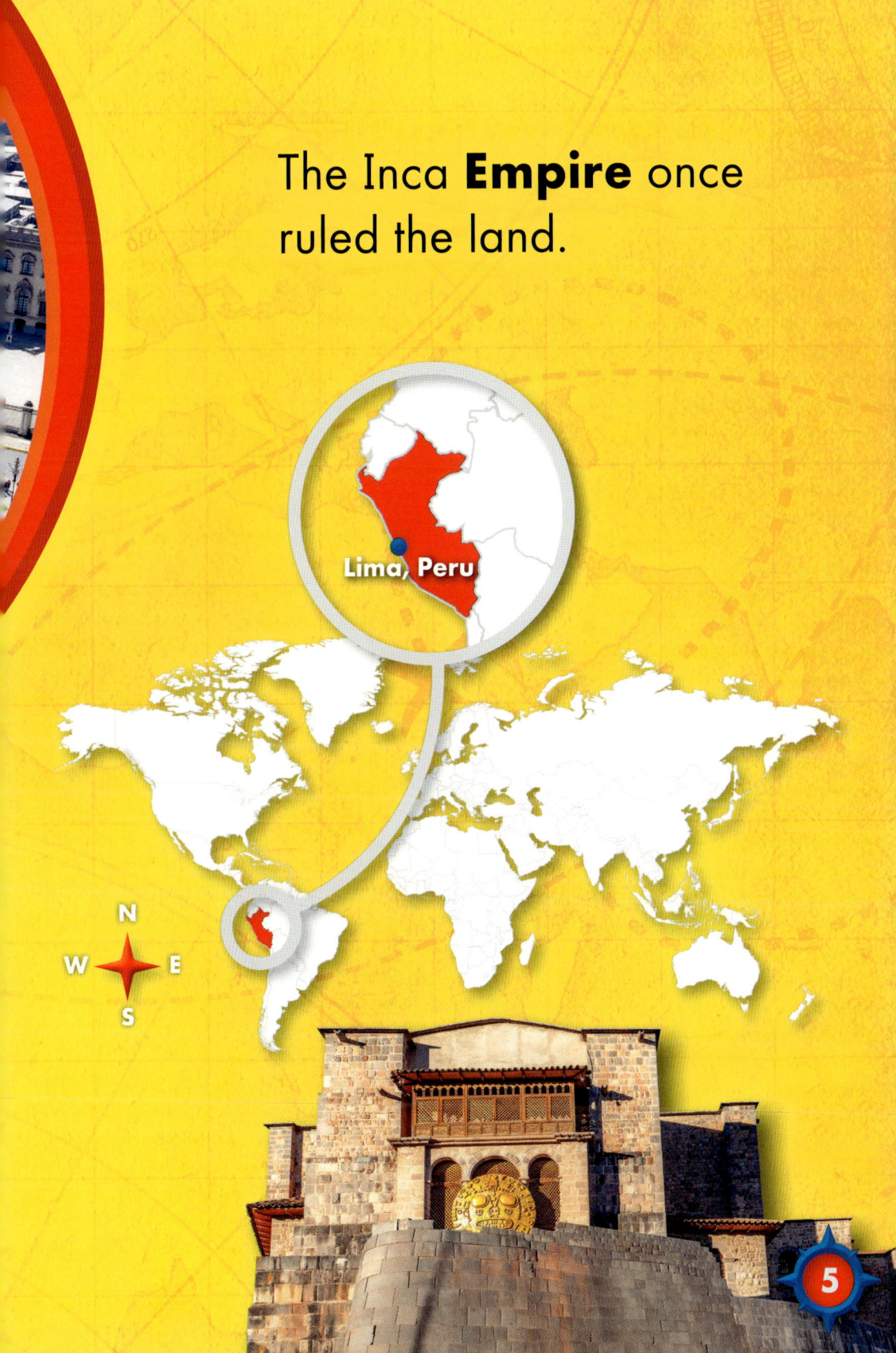

The Inca **Empire** once ruled the land.

Land and Animals

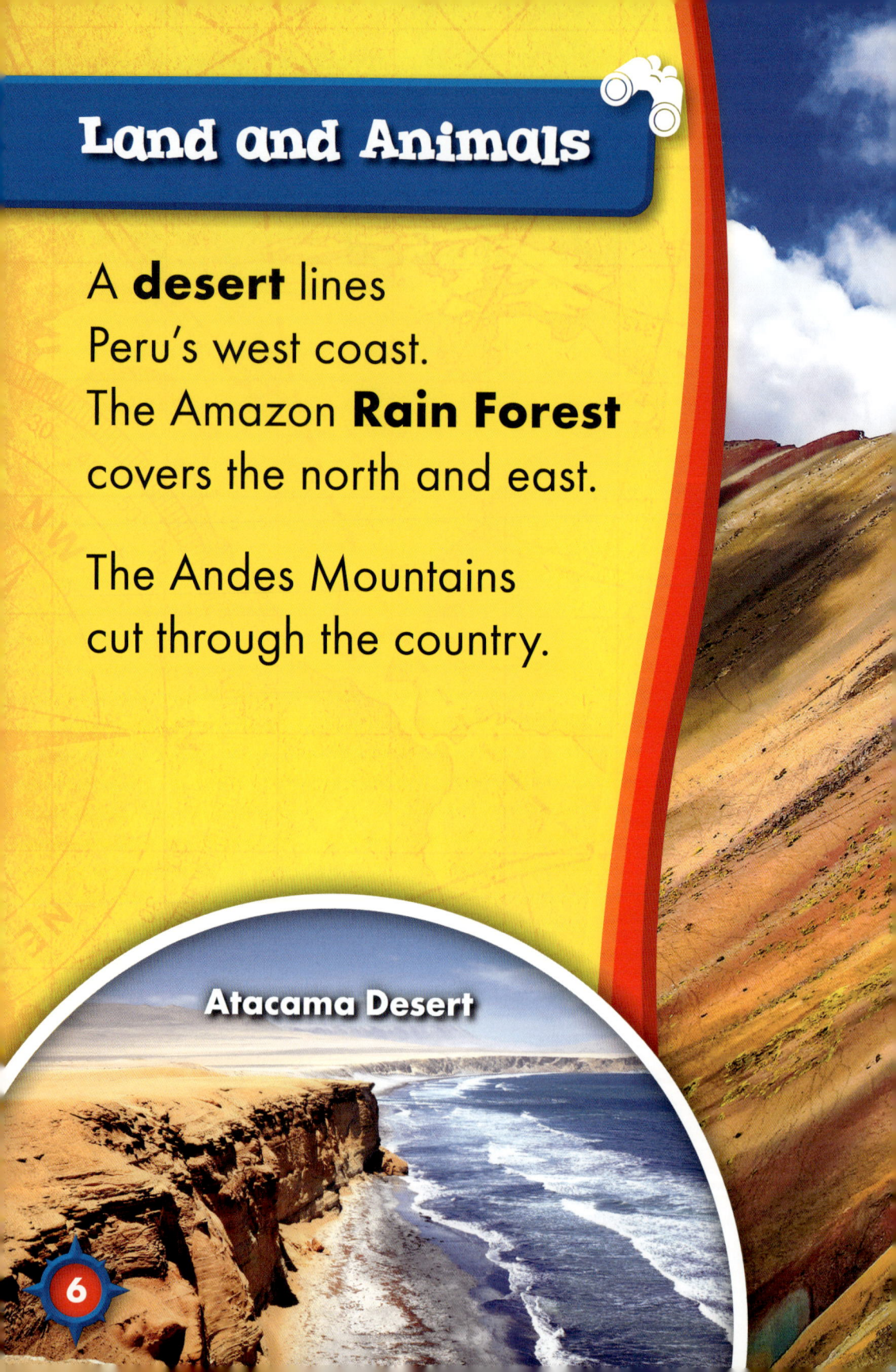

A **desert** lines Peru's west coast. The Amazon **Rain Forest** covers the north and east.

The Andes Mountains cut through the country.

Atacama Desert

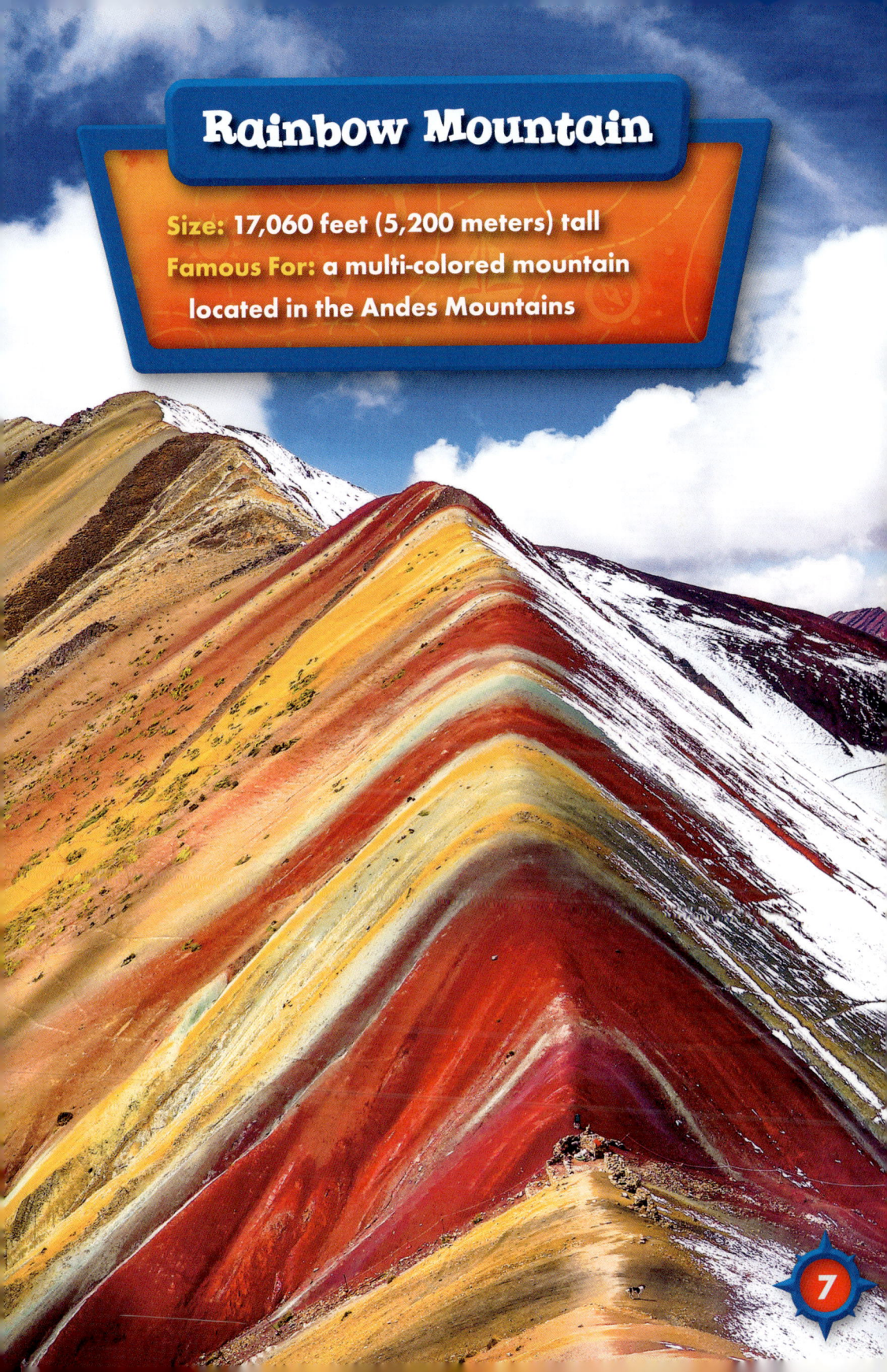

Rainbow Mountain

Size: 17,060 feet (5,200 meters) tall

Famous For: a multi-colored mountain located in the Andes Mountains

Andes Mountains

Western Peru is warm and very dry. It is colder in the mountains.

A lot of rain falls in the Amazon. This rain forest is hot and **humid**.

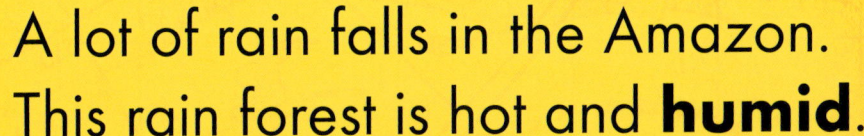

Amazon Rain Forest

Vicuñas climb the mountains. Seabirds fly over the coast. Penguins **waddle** along the shore.

Humboldt penguins

Macaws fly through the rain forest. Caimans swim in the rivers below.

Life in Peru

Peruvians come from many backgrounds. Most speak Spanish. Many are **Catholics**.

People often live in cities near the coast. Lima is the biggest city.

Catholic church

soccer

volleyball

Peruvians enjoy different activities. Soccer is a top sport. People also play volleyball or go surfing.

Large groups attend concerts. They often dance to **traditional** music.

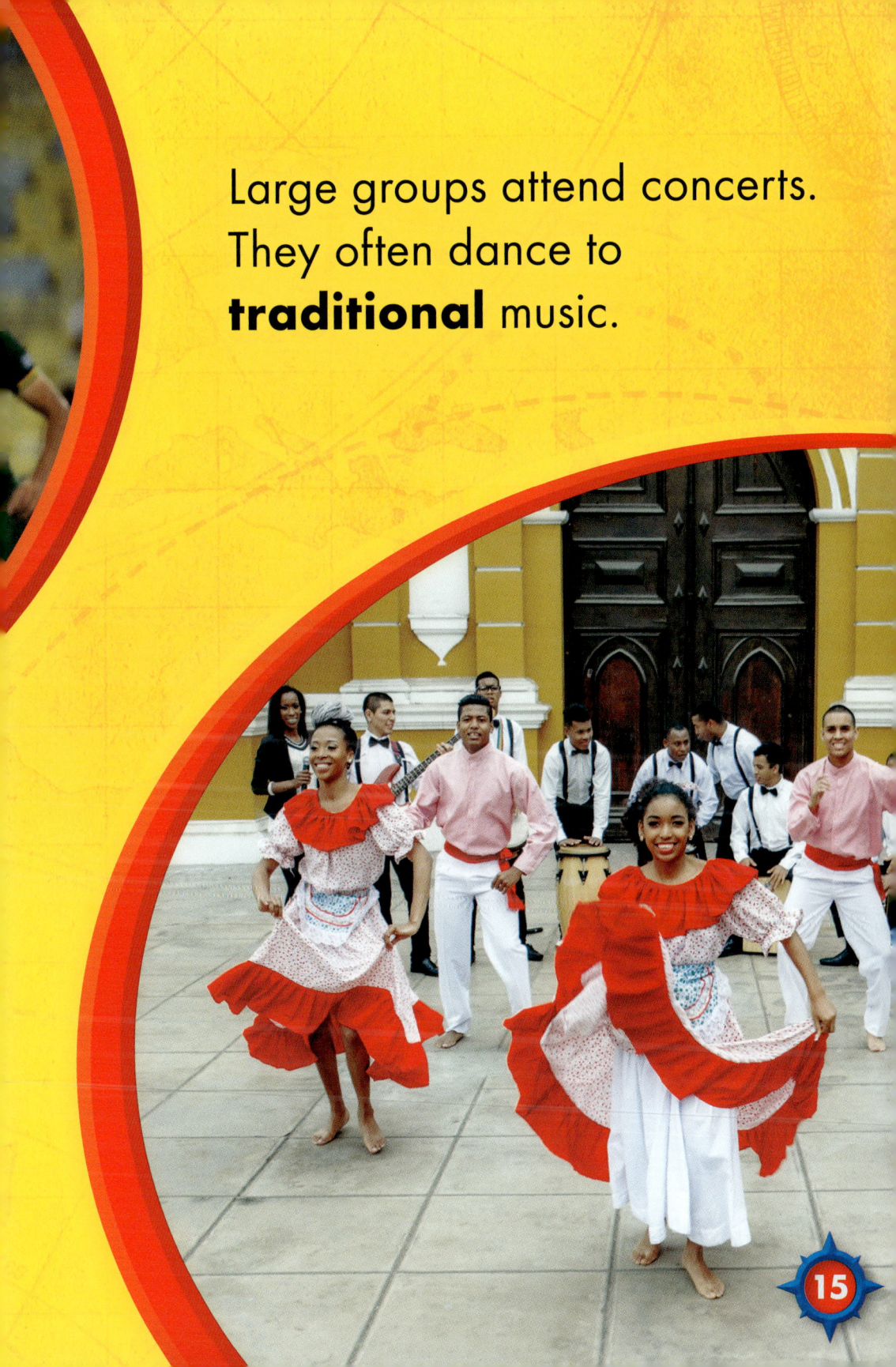

Rice and potatoes are **staples**. Peruvian *ceviche* is a fresh dish of fish and lemon.

Peruvian Foods

ceviche

lomo saltado

picarones

Lomo saltado is stir-fried beef. *Picarones* are sweet doughnuts!

Peru's national holiday is Independence Day. People wave flags and play music.

Semana Santa

Semana Santa is Holy Week. People go to church and eat big meals. Holidays bring Peruvians together!

Peru Facts

Size:
496,225 square miles
(1,285,216 square kilometers)

Population:
32,275,736 (2022)

National Holiday:
Independence Day (July 28)

Main Languages:
Spanish, Quechua, Aymara

Capital City:
Lima

Famous Face

Name: Susan Egoavil

Famous For: national volleyball player

Religions

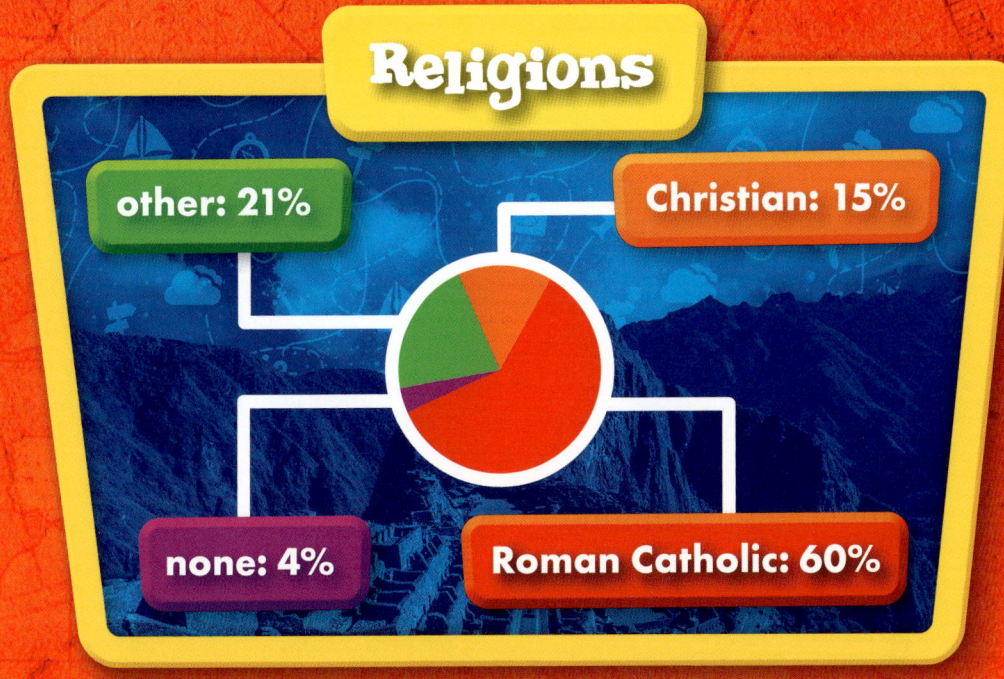

- other: 21%
- Christian: 15%
- none: 4%
- Roman Catholic: 60%

Top Landmarks

Inca Trail

Machu Picchu

Nazca Lines

Glossary

Catholics—people belonging or relating to the Christian church that is led by the pope

desert—dry land with few plants and little rainfall

empire—a government with one ruler that rules over a large number of other places and people

humid—having a lot of water in the air

rain forest—a thick, green forest that receives a lot of rain

staples—widely used foods or other items

traditional—related to the customs, ideas, or beliefs handed down from one generation to the next

waddle—to move with short steps while shifting from side to side

To Learn More

AT THE LIBRARY

Bjorklund, Ruth, and Sloane Gould. *Peru*. New York, N.Y.: Cavendish Square Publishing, 2023.

Hansen, Grace. *Machu Picchu*. Minneapolis, Minn.: Abdo, 2019.

Kenney, Karen Latchana. *Macaws*. Minneapolis, Minn.: Bellwether Media, 2021.

ON THE WEB

Factsurfer.com gives you a safe, fun way to find more information.

1. Go to www.factsurfer.com.
2. Enter "Peru" into the search box and click 🔍.
3. Select your book cover to see a list of related content.

Index

Amazon Rain Forest, 6, 9, 11
Andes Mountains, 6, 8, 10
animals, 10, 11
capital (see Lima)
Catholics, 12
cities, 12
coast, 6, 10, 12
dance, 15
desert, 6
food, 16, 17, 19
Inca Empire, 5
Independence Day, 18
Lima, 4, 5, 12
map, 5
music, 15, 18
Pacific Ocean, 4
people, 12, 14, 18, 19
Peru facts, 20–21
rain, 9
Rainbow Mountain, 7
rivers, 11
say hello, 13
Semana Santa, 19
soccer, 14
South America, 4
Spanish, 12, 13
surfing, 14
volleyball, 14

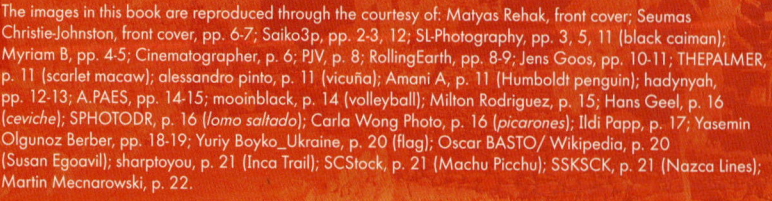

The images in this book are reproduced through the courtesy of: Matyas Rehak, front cover; Seumas Christie-Johnston, front cover, pp. 6-7; Saiko3p, pp. 2-3, 12; SL-Photography, pp. 3, 5, 11 (black caiman); Myriam B, pp. 4-5; Cinematographer, p. 6; PJV, p. 8; RollingEarth, pp. 8-9; Jens Goos, pp. 10-11; THEPALMER, p. 11 (scarlet macaw); alessandro pinto, p. 11 (vicuña); Amani A, p. 11 (Humboldt penguin); hadynyah, pp. 12-13; A.PAES, pp. 14-15; mooinblack, p. 14 (volleyball); Milton Rodriguez, p. 15; Hans Geel, p. 16 (*ceviche*); SPHOTODR, p. 16 (*lomo saltado*); Carla Wong Photo, p. 16 (*picarones*); Ildi Papp, p. 17; Yasemin Olgunoz Berber, pp. 18-19; Yuriy Boyko_Ukraine, p. 20 (flag); Oscar BASTO/ Wikipedia, p. 20 (Susan Egoavil); sharptoyou, p. 21 (Inca Trail); SCStock, p. 21 (Machu Picchu); SSKSCK, p. 21 (Nazca Lines); Martin Mecnarowski, p. 22.